What Love Took,

Karan Bhaip

Copyright © Karan Bhaip
All Rights Reserved.

This book has been self-published with all reasonable efforts taken to make the material error-free by the author. No part of this book shall be used, reproduced in any manner whatsoever without written permission from the author, except in the case of brief quotations embodied in critical articles and reviews.

The Author of this book is solely responsible and liable for its content including but not limited to the views, representations, descriptions, statements, information, opinions and references ["Content"]. The Content of this book shall not constitute or be construed or deemed to reflect the opinion or expression of the Publisher or Editor. Neither the Publisher nor Editor endorse or approve the Content of this book or guarantee the reliability, accuracy or completeness of the Content published herein and do not make any representations or warranties of any kind, express or implied, including but not limited to the implied warranties of merchantability, fitness for a particular purpose. The Publisher and Editor shall not be liable whatsoever for any errors, omissions, whether such errors or omissions result from negligence, accident, or any other cause or claims for loss or damages of any kind, including without limitation, indirect or consequential loss or damage arising out of use, inability to use, or about the reliability, accuracy or sufficiency of the information contained in this book.

Made with ♥ on the Notion Press Platform
www.notionpress.com

Dear Devotees,

If you've ever loved someone with pure devotion, then this book is for you.

To be devoted in love is to get ruined.

To my mother,

Art runs in our blood and I will forever be grateful to you for that.

Forever in my prayers.

This is the sad **DEMISE** of love between you
and me,

Lonesome we run away from one another and I
hope it sets you free.

What Love Took,

Grief is a claustrophobic experience after a heartbreak. These poems are born from that ache, exploring the raw, unspoken polarity of emotions that heartbreak brings. When you lose someone, you deeply loved, you don't just lose them—you lose parts of yourself. The deeper the investment, the more intertwined your identity becomes with theirs. And when they're gone, you're left fragmented, hollow, grappling to find who you are without them.

Heartbreak is a landscape of contrasts: love and hate, well-wishing and cursing, joy and despair. It blurs the edges of perception, leaving you isolated within vivid, overwhelming emotions. You find pieces of yourself scattered in the drawers of love, tucked away in memories you can't quite let go of.

Grieving a love that still lives is harder than grieving one that's passed. The currency of love never loses its value—it remains timeless. This book is that currency, a testament, a memoir, a fragile souvenir from me to my lost love.

INDEX

BONUS POEMS

So raw!

I love the sight of you in the cold wind,

It leaves me with a feeling of warmth within.

The breeze kisses your cheeks out in open,

As my eyes touch your lips and leave you a
token.

You make my heart not pound but put it at
rest,

Out of all my day dreams this one came true
for the best.

My head is all curls but with starred tiara
around them,

Fell flat on face but your arms held back up my
head.

Clearing is the mist from the air as I bathe in
your love,

It brought me colours, tears, clover and a
gracious white dove.

My book, my movie, my film, my memory is
the moment by the metro,

Your smile and innocence are my scenic beauty since the get-go.

And for the first time I was watching someone who's already mine,

When our eyes meet, they tell me everything will be fine.

No more I have to scheme to be the novelty of someone's dream,

I silence my executant and surrender to life of calm; I feel white within.

Oh, to be in love and never fall sick of it ever again,

Flare the flag of harmony and may stand tall our reign.

My honour, my shield, my emblem, my queen,

To you the most than for anyone anything I have ever been.

You are now my religion, my future, my family, my culture,

Please hold onto my soul forever and I promise to fight off your vulture.

Karan Bhaip | What Love Took,

So raw, less sorrow, so tender to keep a dream
of tomorrow,

Hoping to grow together into trees from the
seeds sowed in burrow.

Pour into my cup, the waters from your seas
for some luck,

I will do the same as my arms keep
you safe and snug.

Karan Bhaip | What Love Took,

Love

Love is an alluring garden,

Love is a raging storm.

It's all things big and beautiful,

It's all things dirty and wrong.

Love is a hefty burden,

If you carry, you're strong.

Love is a pearl in the soft palms,

Like sand, it slips if gripped wrong.

It could be found on many faces,

As flush, as tears or in the shape of fears.

When it comes to you, do keep it warm,

Don't you gamble love, it will be gone.

Love can be angelic sounds from the harp,

Pull the strings wrong and summon an eternal scar.

Don't you mishandle the petals of love,

Let them bloom, the tender feathers of dove.

Karan Bhaip | What Love Took,

Braided souls

Two souls braided in one,

Like fire and air—look how wild they burn!

Water brings emotion of peace,

While winter wraps sun's tension with ease.

Universe brings us close to the balance,

Two lovers engulfed in the rhythm of ballad.

She wears them with pride like a crown,

Arms wrapped like flower garlands around.

Beautiful us

The town talked about us,

They loved the way I loved.

I was happy in loving you,

Your company was my favourite too.

Your smile brightened my day,

My demons simply faded away.

My spirits were yellow high,

I loved how you'd colour my sky.

Our faces looked the same,

Like twins we lost in one another's gaze.

You made metro trains more romantic,

Something about you and me was poetic.

Your past protested as bystander,

But our love paraded over the sonder.

I wish I could sing you our song,

Rings made of paper on our fingers around.

My lover, my love for you is deep as the ocean,

Our album, our photos of memories are now
not in motion.

Our gypsies couldn't stand the wind,

Grievance of our love now lives within.

Karan Bhaip | What Love Took,

Echoes of lost love

I'm a voyeur to your ocean now watching you
far from my shore,

Nothing beats the life I lived for almost 3
months in our lore.

These days I depend on a glass of dark amber
whiskey,

Gulping it neat hoping it will wash away our
tragic history.

Yesterday I got some cigarettes when I felt I've
lost myself at the hem,

Don't want my lips to touch them, I felt lonely
and mad so I brought them.

I find myself again choking by the smoke of
our phantom fires,

I wake up from sleep with burns on my heart it
has lost its desire.

Thinking it back, I believe you breaking up
with me was for your best,

My depression would've ruined you as well
just like it has annihilated my nest.

Karan Bhaip | What Love Took,

Yes, you were hurtful and I gave you my most and my good,

But when you left, I felt like I've lost myself again in the depths of the woods.

My cup is now broken and empty so it makes hateful noises,

I know that you hate those but they come from the spilled us.

If you ever look at the spill closely, you'll see how much you still mean to me,

You are my roses, my gypsies, my sunflowers and you are what I only see.

I know that the candle of your passion and infatuation has burned out,

You'll find my love scraping off the wax off the floor since our fallout.

Deep red rose petals on my sight hold back the dew drops of my eyes,

I love you; I miss you, I'm sorry, I forgive you are the words on paper planes lost in the skies.

I think to myself that we unfolded magically and tragically for a reason,

Karan Bhaip | What Love Took,

Fate saw it in premonition that I become your future-lasting burden.

So, I'm not surprised that fate and you took you away from me,

I was a burden to them and wouldn't want it to be yours so destiny set you free.

Karan Bhaip | What Love Took,

(EXTENDED)

I'm a voyeur to your newly found change and your happiness,

If you have any hurt from me left, I claim it back as my mess.

May you grow and may you be the happiest in your life,

I promise I won't be bitter towards your success even though you're not mine.

I hope all the words that hurt you from me have healed by now,

If not then I hope you hear my apologies in your sleep as my song.

I forgive you too my ex-lover for all the hurt you have laid in me that I harbour,

We're young and we have lost, hope we will grow through this heart burn.

Karan Bhaip | What Love Took,

Turmoil

I don't think I'm being dramatic when I say
you're demolishing me,

You don't see that you're hurting me every time
you take their names.

I know you're mine but your cold shoulder has
frozen my mind,

As I be the soldier and put efforts for you, you
bring him up again,

You bring him up right after your cold replies
and I lose my mind.

I'm trying my hard to ignore it but you just
don't get it,

When you do it, it hurts me and demolishes me
a bit by bit.

I have never cried in a broad daylight but now
my eyes leak every morning,

Every drop my tears shed my fear grows and
intensifies it.

I know by your pattern that you're going to
leave me and fly for the next.

You told me I was different, I was special than them, don't make me your new regret.

Make me feel that assurance which you've given me in written.

Make me feel the trust on you and take away my fears left unspoken,

I only wish to love you for evermore and not see you in tears.

I hope we heal and you feel for me again let's rise above our fears.

Karan Bhaip | What Love Took,

The wreck!

Fill your love in my cup, can you do it for me please?

With each and every soft kiss from mine onto your lips.

Bite the edge and leak some venom off your teeth.

Can you put me to ease? Can you help my soul release?

I keep telling you it's just not this one thing,

It's a pile of many little things of everything.

I don't keep the scoreboard in my heart,

But my mind can pull them out from the dark.

If you ask me what exactly did you do?

I might not answer then, but Love, it's all true.

Out of sight from my eyes when you'll go,

All of it will run in my mind but you'll never know.

Karan Bhaip | What Love Took,

Space needs to stay blank please keep it that
way,

If you walk in my direction, will I choose the
other way?

I don't understand my Love, where all of this is
going,

But without trying I don't think there is a way
of knowing.

The petals 'round our flowers are now wilting,

And we are not waking yet my heart is aching.

Streams of river might run down our faces,

They'll dry out but will leave behind lasting
traces.

I don't know what could help to build us back,

Maybe if we can cut ourselves some slack.

It's coming, I fear. It's faster I swear.

It's here, it's here. The final wreck is near.

Karan Bhaip | What Love Took,

Shattered And Unravelled, Rising Above Vows

Did you knock on my door looking red and severely wounded?

For a moment of shelter? A home you had founded?

I healed your wounds and hugged your spine warm,

As you froze mine and let it snap with your sad around.

I burned myself to grey ashes to bring you the light,

You blew my grey dust and my ghost caught your long sigh.

Time has now passed and it's been almost 100 days,

I have a factual perspective about February the 3rd haze.

I see you now for who you are instead of seeing the man I had made,

Karan Bhaip | What Love Took,

I was right all along and you fumbled me till
my sanity was erased.

Your letters on the doorstep of your ex-lover
were caught,

You called it a reflex and made me say sorry
after I had fought.

Are you having fun now with your 9th
wonderland?

Telling him your sob stories and pulling him in
your dreamland?

Do you pour him with love, dream and care
just to snatch it away?

Are you making him run behind you until he
loses himself on his way.

Is he trying to love you and help you to get out
of the woods?

Tell him the plot where you will deprive him of
love and leave for his good.

Karan Bhaip | What Love Took,

Oh no! I now have so much perspective that I wisely contain,

Could weave all the truth in my poems but I chose to restrain.

You used me as I bent myself unconditionally around your heart,

The damage I suffer is incomprehensible for your shallow smart.

And by smart, I mean your mind that has no considering thought,

You are only considerate to your own self and never learn the lessons taught.

Do you sit alone and listen to all your gospel songs?

Are they loud enough to turn the volume of your thoughts down?

May Jesus bring you the perspective of how you killed me every day,

He saw me weep in the shadow of his cross for you with every passing day.

Karan Bhaip | What Love Took,

Now I pray to him for myself and for helping
me to stay away from your mess,

Even though my hands fell off praying for your
wellness and goodness.

Karan Bhaip | What Love Took,

Battlefield

Let's get down and dirty in the ring, in the mud pit,

Like two bulls fighting one another as if it is all worth it.

Let's make a mess on the ground, let's cause a havoc now,

We both have nothing to lose, let's go bad and break this clock and my vow.

Let's hug our prides and our egos instead of quitting games,

Let's play till we both ruin both of us with our claims and our blames.

I don't know about you but I still love you even though it chokes,

I hope hearing this makes you feel validated but don't keep any hopes.

Am I ready to get swindled by your charm again? I'm not.

I don't want to make you a villain again of my dreams until we rot.

Don't try to communicate again with a hi that
is sent-unsent,

You meant the world to me but I have to put
this chaos to an end.

Karan Bhaip | What Love Took,

Wall

You have to hate me from your heart till the core,

Because until you don't, I will love you for evermore.

If you try to come back, I will just take you in,

And I fear what will happen when I do that again.

My arms are always open to give you my shelter,

So, I want you to be the one who never tries to enter.

Time will heal me and my sacred love for you will fade,

Keeping you in and around my life wouldn't be of any aid.

So go ahead and create a wall that must remain unbreakable,

Because I know your cannonballs will break my walls and I will stay breakable.

Demise

Put me in the list of one of your regrets,

Pass me the curse and make it your best one yet.

I will go back to writing the poems so raw,

While I contemplate here sitting in my sorrow.

You have been nice and dirty all through and through,

Let your fears consume all of us and yourself too.

You do dirty to guys who are so young and kind.

Like you did to the guy whose name is same as mine.

You poured your whole ocean for the guy with white oud.

While he drowned you in the same waters like we knew he would.

And when the time came to love a man made of good,

You lacked in every way and drained out my love as much as you could.

You never intended to do me so bad and so dirty,

But you were getting bored is what you told me.

My affection became the noose around your neck so you hurt me,

My love was making you insufferable as I gave too much is what you told me.

This is my way of trying to cope with my sadness,

It's one of my classics to put up a show off my madness.

Now here I'm am alone sitting at the top of an acacia tree,

Watching below all the flooded memories looking not so pretty.

You were neither capable to take my love nor strong enough to take my hate,

So, it's better if I be nice and let it all go or forever your heart will ache.

Karan Bhaip | What Love Took,

Oh, now don't blame me for seeking external sympathy,

When I was yours, you failed giving me your empathy.

This is the sad **DEMISE** of love between you and me,

Lonesome we run away from one another and I hope it sets you free.

Karan Bhaip | What Love Took,

Sad slow ballad

Life is like a sad slow ballad,

Orchestral violins in the back.

The kind of song that gives you heartache,

The kind that makes you want to replay it
again.

The strings sound deep as the plot gets thick,

Cutting the soft fingers tips, the blood bleeds
rich.

My poetries are my catharsis, they paint my
beauty,

Alluring the talks of the town, I tell them my
story like it's my duty.

I share my sacred honour, I share my disgrace,

All these things come back and blow up on my
face.

The melancholic living won't rescue me from
the flat,

The ways I pull myself above the valleys,
proud pats on my back.

Karan Bhaip | What Love Took,

Life is like a burning house of dreams,

Flames dance in the ashes of screams.

Karan Bhaip | What Love Took,

Dead end

I'm standing face to face yet again with the
biggest blue wall,

All those times I have growled so loud it had
fallen back down.

But this time it's different, I can tell that it's a
dead end,

I've reached out for every help, but this time
there's no hope lend.

They ask me to break the wall again like it's not
insurmountable,

Living a life of surviving and struggling has
made breathing disable.

It's so funny that I'd fight for everyone I love
and care about,

But I won't fight for myself through this agony
and find a way out.

Every day is a dark night without a moon and
stars in my sky,

I wish to set my soul free, let the wings break
out from spine and fly high.

Karan Bhaip | What Love Took,

With every breath, a tear holds itself back from
crashing down my face,

I ask destiny, I beg and I pled to put down
the pen and erase.

Karan Bhaip | What Love Took,

Inner conflict

Shaking my leg as the anxiety attacks my system again,

Craving for something very sweet to calm with sugar in my vein.

I don't like dressing up the way I used to before and go out,

I want to shut myself away from everyone and by them be forgot.

No longer I feel like a human who functions well, I'm mundane,

My train runs on every possible track but they all lead to bane.

I envision laptop wire like necklace, paint brushes for my eyes,

Living with the feelings of longing and yearning is what I despise.

My mind is walking in a dessert and without water it's trembling,

Any sight of false mirage could help me to push myself and keep going.

Karan Bhaip | What Love Took,

There's a lack of colour in my spirit and so I see myself in Grey,

I want to scream as I ascend into madness, predatory lunacy and I'm its prey.

Karan Bhaip | What Love Took,

The Last Page

I see everything in the scales of Grey.

This shade feels so wrong, I'm its prey.

My rage rains on a White Blank Page,

My eyes leak on my phone screen in pain.

The lost hair will grow back with time,

Once I lose my mind, I won't stay sublime.

My virtues feel like my biggest enemy and my crime,

They came back to me as vices from the man I once called mine.

Breathing-battling-winning is my transgression,

The holy trinity has failed in peace ingression.

My broken bones are refusing the mending,

Is this The Last Page with a pitch black ending?

The town talks again about the fires I carry as I try to put off within,

The answer to my every thought starts with the stopping of breathing.

Karan Bhaip | What Love Took,

All Too Wells and all too sads are leading me to
the dead end,

I reached for the light from the gods but they
dismissed my hand.

Love-Therapy-Pills failed to fix my broken
parts,

I'm all over the floor like the blood spilled art.

I look to the sky with The Last Page in my
hands,

I ask the forces to write a merciful fate with
a beautiful end.

Karan Bhaip | What Love Took,

Put me to ease

My dear mother, take me away with you,

Life on this earth only seems to get cruel.

Living without light feels like imprisonment,

I never thought I'd be the one to get abandoned.

I try to poke my head out of the drowning water,

But the blues of the sea keeps me anchored.

Can your hand reach out to me and cut my spine?

Let the wings of my soul break out free so that I can fly.

The smoke seems to never leave my lungs alone,

Infiltrating the roots of them it keeps me chocked.

Come here mother please visit to me in my dreams,

Tell me everything with be worthy and I will breathe clean.

Karan Bhaip | What Love Took,

Hug me in the field of dreams and ease me,

Skipping in the landscapes I'll live
alone and be free.

Karan Bhaip | What Love Took,

Tousled head

On the ground are falling the bricks of my future,

I can't stand the building where I'm not the bright one,

Feeling like academics of life is murder and crime.

Have been circling in the system and now up is my time.

I wish to have peace but my mind screams in chaos.

I derailed my own railway off every track I could have.

Neck deep down I try to breathe half vulnerable underground.

Dying of thirst to be heard and understood by someone close.

They all listen standing around but the void in my heart is not shut.

Nobody is at home it's vacant and it's loud in the quiet.

Karan Bhaip | What Love Took,

Want to feel dear again to someone, want to
feel human.

Breathing in and out while smoke fill my lungs,
I just want to withdraw.

Karan Bhaip | What Love Took,

Let go white horse!

The real face of Love was terrible,

When the skin fell off it was unbearable.

The fireworks are just smoke that chokes,

Shines the sky for a while and then it does a
backstroke.

The air that smelled like white oud,

Does nothing more now but give me brain fog.

Your indifference is a big punch in my gut,

But I say it's shit and shows you didn't care
much.

The ones who think indifference is wise,

Are those who avoid showing where their care
lies.

Bury me, all of me since you got tired already,

My storms don't think for me you are ready.

I am a poison when wronged who kills a little
by little,

Run away from me before I fire off the
suppressed missile.

Karan Bhaip | What Love Took,

I demanded your patience but it was over
looked,

You say you love me but not necessarily I feel
to the most,

My forced comfort, my home, my love, my
hopes.

I clanged onto the potential of feeling all those.

This revelation from my therapy was scary to
me,

Because I realized I was in love which wasn't
for me.

I hate to think that because I was in love with
you so deeply,

I would've read my vows smiling bright at you
so nonchalantly.

Now that we are broken branches, I think it is
best to know,

I'm saying thank you boy for letting
your white horse go.

Karan Bhaip | What Love Took,

A wish

Dear to me you are my beloved,

Where are you now?

How's your life been?

I don't need to know any of that,

But my love is still eager and keen.

You are a kind man to the world,

Only kind to them not for both of us.

You do deserve happiness and joy,

But in sorrow your comfort resides.

I hope your life gets a chance to rejoice.

Don't hide under the table,

Don't turn your back from the light.

I was unkind to you at your worst,

Only because I felt like I had no other choice.

I'm truly sorry my love to call you cursed.

Karan Bhaip | What Love Took,

Please know that I'm all yours,

Though I can't stay with you.

Pink and purple are faded for tonight,

My shooting star won't fall in your sky again.

I pray that it wouldn't but it just might.

Karan Bhaip | What Love Took,

A week away

You blew off the candles of our 3 months cake
when it was just a week away,

And left me celebrating it with your ghost in
the darkness, I thought you'd stay.

I made a fool of me with the gifts and chocolate
covered strawberries,

Your angelic eyes looking in my siren sights
which I thought we mutually cherished.

Here I am babe standing, still counting months
and days I kept my promise.

It's 31st of May but how can I be happy when
my longing speak about the way I miss.

If I look into your eyes again, would they
sparkle because of me?

You said I was forever stuck with you then
why did you let go so easily?

My mind still ponders upon our love affair
asking if it was a punishment?

If it was then had I paid all my karmic debt
because I'm now a tired man.

Karan Bhaip | What Love Took,

Blindsided

My hard-earned years of confidence you shattered,

My self-esteem corroded for us but it did not matter.

Your shallow sorry couldn't undo the stabs in my heart,

As the wounds bled kind and pure blood you left leaving me to fall apart.

I will forget and I will do better and there will be a time when this wouldn't matter,

But till the fires of my death bed, I will carry the stains of this aching love affair.

You left me saying your numb heart was the reason,

But here we go again with your new 9th toy in the same season.

My spring of a heart collapsed when your invisible storms collided,

The irony between you leaving me and getting a new toy hit me blindsided.

Karan Bhaip | What Love Took,

The way life goes

Love will come back on its own,

Don't grieve the loss just let it all go.

Loosen up the grip of the chokehold,

Warm up from hues of sad, it has been cold.

The call ended a long time ago,

So, rest your hand now, don't hold onto the phone.

Get out of the dark and live all alone,

Embrace yourself and know yourself more.

That's just the way life goes,

Don't you drown yourself in your woes!

Life might not stay forever this cold,

You will get better when you're old.

So don't you worry about the rain,

Dance through the storms even when in pain.

The sun will shine bright and dry off your clothes,

That's just the way life unfolds.

Karan Bhaip | What Love Took,

Misery business

There's beauty in agony if you see it closely,

Or am I just trying to see the best in my
misery?

Searching for the good in terribly rotten mess,

So that I don't lose my last hope and my breath.

Sleeping on the floor bare naked on my chest,

Ten swords upright standing still on my back.

The metamorphosis has only just begun,

Life has its way of wrecking and building the
fun.

I welcome the new change with my arms wide
open,

I will become more stronger and sharper than
stay broken.

My name is Karan Bhaip, my resilience gives
them the frights,

I develop thickest skin, outwards and within,
and I know how to fight.

I've come this far by putting all the work, tears
and love,

I won't give up and back down now in the time
of woe.

I have given my everything in living this life,

It's time for it to pay back with a fortune that's
mine.

It was a karmic misery business but it shall
turn golden now,

I've paid for all my wrongs and my sins; it's
time to win now.

Karan Bhaip | What Love Took,

For once and for all

For once I don't just want to survive,

I want to feel young and alive.

Taste the happiness,

Hear the beauty of life,

Soak in the grace without torment,

Not drown but float in the wind and the wild.

There shall be a victory to be celebrated,

Without any fear of losing myself all again.

See the glory of the sunrise,

Smell the fragrant queen of night,

For once I'd like to keep good things for me.

Yellow and blue are the guests who come and
go,

I'd like if yellow stays back with me at my
home.

I don't want to find myself all alone,

For once and for all, I want someone who
chooses not to go.

Karan Bhaip | What Love Took,

Love like a woman

I learned to love like a woman from my own mother,

Saw her pour herself unconditional to fill the family's cup.

Till the final drop she poured and poured until she dried out,

She waited for the summer rain to fill her happiness back up.

The summer rain never came it only always stormed,

Until the vessel of her heart stopped, she never had herself anything good found.

Then I got loved by a woman from another part of the world,

We never got to meet but I swear she loved me so much.

She was a woman in love and I was a boy back then,

Karan Bhaip | What Love Took,

She sent me a card from abroad risking everything she had.

I felt and took all her love and I failed to give any of it back,

Because I was a boy broken seated alone in my own mess.

Now it was me who loved someone that much for the first time,

And hence I get why women in love make their partner their religion.

I used to scold my mother for being the way she was,

Because the world too harsh sucked out her kindness and benefited off.

I became like them but I got to learn my lesson on time,

Now I know when and how much to give a lover all of mine.

Karan Bhaip | What Love Took,

The lesson here I learnt is to keep my love for
lover unconditional,

But before that I should love myself and
receive the same non-conditional.

Women's love remains superior so learn to love
like a woman,

Him, her or someone other it doesn't matter
when you love like a woman.

Remember a teaching that if someone wants to
then they will,

The strength, courage and tenderness needed
in love will show you, their will.

Karan Bhaip | What Love Took,

I am

I am bright as the sunflower,

I'm delicate as the baby's breath.

I'm soft as the feather,

I am calm as the Queen's Necklace breeze.

Hold me in your memory.

I am nice and kind as Taylor Swift,

I try being poetic but not as Walt Whitman.

I'm golden and sweet as the honey,

I'm strong as the currents of the sea.

Hold me in the waters of your memory.

When I was sixteen,

Maybe a year little more.

I took the worst hit.

Survived it all alone,

Now look at the things I've accomplished.

Karan Bhaip | What Love Took,

Soon I'll be a year older than twenty-one,

People think I have had a lot of fun.

But I still take those hits,

Grace, I show despite of it.

My soul is pure and that's the
legacy they relish.

Ghosts and phantoms

The ghosts and phantoms of my virtues whisper to me,

That the strength I seek from around already resides within me.

The age-old sword in my hands is no longer needed,

Bury it in the ground and look around, all evil has already faded.

There's no battle or sickness on the war field left to conquer,

Shall not now peace sleep in my palms? I caught her.

Yet I dig my fingers in the ground in search of empathy,

All the dirt and peelings of skin could prove to be worthy.

I need to believe the good I give and contain within me,

Cannot afford to let the invaders infiltrate my mind and me.

No longer I need the receipt of my goodness
shoved on my face to believe,

I keep faith on my own self now and with
grace and tender heart I live.

Karan Bhaip | What Love Took,

Virtue of my voices

It was my grave, your gun.

You ran to find a new one.

There will be time,

When I will sit and sip wine.

Each sip when you take the hit,

You get the karma for what you did.

Every tear you made me shed,

The pages of our book, ink only bled.

Your ink through my veins burst out in pain.

I will wait to watch the karmic debt you'll pay.

Ceramic pitcher of your sins is full to the brim.

If you sit to confess the way you sin,

A confessional booth would be your prison
cell.

May someday in your mind rings perspective's
bell.

Hope you stop your romance hunt and not kill
more people,

Karan Bhaip | What Love Took,

Leaving behind us impaired, you are what is
why we cripple.

You dragged me to hell with the view of sky
with you,

Left me there to seek new thrill and new
adventure for your breakthrough.

I suffer now for all the wrong choices,

I should've surrendered to virtue of my voices.

Karan Bhaip | What Love Took,

Drawers of our love

It feels so good to finally have myself back,

With the help of my pills, I put my fires at rest.

Had forgotten how much my shine was
sublime,

Reciting all my attempts of saving myself, I'm
no longer blind.

Each time I was wrecked by the strong currents
of the sea,

My winds charmed along and chimed in to set
myself out free.

Long gone are the days when I'd get lost in
someone's haze,

Walk myself out while trying to run on their
twisted paths of maze.

I'm alone, on my own and there's nothing
satisfying for my soul.

Lone fox walking on the road of fiery ashes, oh
I feel so grown.

May my eyes be able to rain but only after right
summer days,

Karan Bhaip | What Love Took,

Only if the showers that helped the field blossom are being embraced.

It has taken blood, sweat and tears to work the magic up on my terrain,

I reckon to witness my landscape is one's privilege and gain.

Shall I always fall apart to put myself back together?

Is strong resilience paying the cost that's inherent from my mother?

In denial I searched for him in the shade and shadow of the cross,

Found myself out and within when I figured my grievance wasn't his loss.

Stake drove right through the centre of my heart,

I took it out to heal the pain then the rivers of blood turned into my art.

I ran so fast when the 100th time you pushed me away to fall apart,

Rummaging through the drawers of our love to find a reason to stay as your part.

Karan Bhaip | What Love Took,

Sweet escape

I dream about landscapes and the wide skies,

In my mind they look beautiful and pretty nice.

Though I can't reach the stars in the night sky,

I still bathe and soak my body in the
moonlight.

Never had or found a pot full of golden
pennies,

I dream of laying under sky with dancing
above Borealis.

A garden in summer, pink plaid picnic blanket,

Jam and butter on bread, a wooden fruit
basket.

With flowers in my hand, love the way sun
glares,

Self-love notes written; healing is spiritual
funfair.

Adrianne Lenker on the radio, bees flying in
air,

Humming softly "anything", I found peace rare.

I dream about buildings of history and mystery,

Petite I feel in front of the architectural victory.

My mind travels there from every now and then,

I want to be there bad, but only God knows when.

Never had a chance to see the beautiful world,

I wish to the shooting stars to take me somewhere really far.

Karan Bhaip | What Love Took,

BONUS POEMS

Antithetical lovelorn

So why am I mourning the loss that was not mine?

When I was the one who walked away in plain sight.

He was the devil with flowers all around to whom I'd lose.

I know I had to let go of the road half build and had to choose.

Maybe, it's my impulses begging for swift gratification,

Or maybe his love who held me on Sunday lead your eviction.

But I'm sorry for hunting down your guarded butterflies,

I know it won't change a thing but I pray to God to keep your smile.

The honesty that I give doesn't make me a good person,

Because honesty served cold is only cruelty that aches and worsen.

Karan Bhaip | What Love Took,

I gave up the midway and too soon, I know, I know.

But my smile touched my eyes with him so I had to go.

A pile of mess is me ready to take the risk and run with him,

Fears and fog from the start with him but I can't ignore his grin.

I'm taken once again by the Devil but this time he kept me in,

It's worth the risk I'd say while I love him with some sadness within.

I did want and prayed to God for us to be a thing, sweet souls in golden,

The bracelets woven for us got home after from you I was stolen.

I think the crazy in me connected with the feral rush of his,

I dropped all my guards and caution to fulfil my impulsive wish.

Things wouldn't change we both know but again I'm so sorry to let you go,

Karan Bhaip | What Love Took,

My mind is dreaming clouds on level 9 but my heart has some sorrow.

Forgive me for the ache I put in you by the ache in me,

It's tragic how things turned out so in front of you my poem is down on knees.

Karan Bhaip | What Love Took,

Janvi

Does she know she's much more than 5'8?

Taller and stronger she writes her own fate.

Smarter than any girl I have ever seen or met,

The eyes of her knowledge just go and gets.

Beauty lies in the way she sees the world,

And so, the world brings the beauty back to her.

I know it in my heart that her life is a work of art,

Someday she'll look back and make sense of those scars.

The loving home she wants I know she will create,

Keeping it warm and soft, every corner will illuminate.

There is no force stopping her from achieving success,

As a short-lived friend, I wish her my tender best.

Karan Bhaip | What Love Took,

Finally, she is a poem and not just a sad poet,

A goddess and not just an angel with torn flesh.

She has transformed into the strength of
divinity,

The kindness she extends may it live for
infinity.

Oh Janvi, I am a short-lived friend who's
fleeting,

Behold this poem and it will hold you, to you
my last greeting.

Karan Bhaip | What Love Took,

Friends

I'm rich but no not in the way you'd think,

I have friends who worth more than anything.

They're the beauty my eyes love to seek,

They're the books my mind likes to read.

What we have is too pure to be true,

I pinch myself and their love gets me through.

They're warm as a cup of coffee after a
hangover,

They're red as roses of a bouquet handed over.

Not the birds of a feather yet we flock together,

Bided by the bond no time could leave tattered.

No, we are not lovers but we love
unconditional,

To one another we hold warm, it's so
devotional.

It's the type of love that doesn't haunt you,

Even when they're not around it holds you.

Karan Bhaip | What Love Took,

It's so calm that our stomachs are not all knots,
no doubting if they love me or they love me
not.

No need to test with the trust falls, we just fall,

One of the angels spread wings with just one
call.

They're the best apples of my eye's basket,

With them in my life I fear no death's casket.

The nurturer is nurtured here in our house,

I miss them so much I find them in no crowd.

Yes, I am rich but now in the way you think.

Karan Bhaip | What Love Took,

Acknowledgements

To The Leftovers (Ajay, Komal, Pratham, Jaaee, Shamika, Sakshi, and Tapsee):

Thank you so much for lending me your ears when I needed you the most. I'm grateful to you all for always having my back. I love you with my whole heart.

To Manasi J:

I miss the brainstorming sessions with you at the department library and fantasizing about fan events. I'm grateful to you for always being there like an elder sister—I do the crisis, and you do the management. Thank you!

To Jette:

The woman who loved me when I was an immature boy—your love will always remain superior.

To my friends at MU (Neramay, Sanika, Ayushi, Sakshi, and others):

Thank you for your personal, academic, and professional support. I truly appreciate it.

To Palakshi:

Without you, I wouldn't have survived MU, my Master's, or life. You're my favourite blessing from destiny, and I'm honoured to have you as my friend. Thank you, Palakshi.

To myself:

You've done it, soldier! You've made it through gracefully and with a lot of dignity. Stay strong, and always keep writing.

Karan Bhaip | What Love Took,

www.ingramcontent.com/pod-product-compliance
Lightning Source LLC
Chambersburg PA
CBHW020501160726
47991CB00007B/2762